D0067992

PUTTING
**PLAN
B**
INTO
ACTION

PUTTING
PLAN
B
INTO
ACTION

WHEN GOD DOESN'T SHOW UP
THE WAY YOU THOUGHT HE WOULD

Participant's Guide

PETE WILSON

THOMAS NELSON
Since 1798

NASHVILLE   DALLAS   MEXICO CITY   RIO DE JANEIRO

© 2011 Pete Wilson

All rights reserved. No portion of this book may be reproduced, stored in a retrieval system, or transmitted in any form or by any means—electronic, mechanical, photocopy, recording, scanning, or other—except for brief quotations in critical reviews or articles, without the prior written permission of the publisher.

Published in Nashville, Tennessee, by Thomas Nelson. Thomas Nelson is a registered trademark of Thomas Nelson, Inc.

The publisher is grateful to Dawn Sherill for her writing assistance and collaboration in developing the content for this guide.

Quotes and excerpts have been taken from the trade book version of Plan B © 2009 by Pete Wilson. Used by permission. All rights reserved.

Thomas Nelson, Inc. titles may be purchased in bulk for educational, business, fund-raising, or sales promotional use. For information, please e-mail SpecialMarkets@ThomasNelson.com.

All Scripture quotations are taken from the New Century Version®. © 2005 by Thomas Nelson, Inc. Used by permission. All rights reserved.

Putting Plan B into Action Participant's Guide

ISBN: 978-1-4185-4610-6

Printed in the United States of America

11 12 13 14 15 QG 5 4 3 2 1

CONTENTS

Introduction 1

How to Use This Guide 5

Session 1: Everyone Needs Healing 7

Session 2: The Illusion of Control 25

Session 3: What Is God Doing? 45

Session 4: Me Too 65

Session 5: Unanswered Questions 83

Session 6: The Cross 103

INTRODUCTION

If you're like so many people I know, your shattered dreams may have left you wondering if God is still actively involved in your life. You may wonder if he even cares or if you're too broken and bruised to be healed by him. You probably wonder quite a lot about what to do next.

No matter what has happened or how you feel, please know you're not alone. Because here's what I've been learning: everyone needs healing. Everyone.

Everyone has shattered dreams.

Every one of us has been let down and disappointed in one way or another.

And every one of us needs healing for our brokenness.

Everyone.

We all have this picture of the way our lives should be. And for some of us the picture of the way our lives should be and the picture of reality are just a reminder our lives are not turning out the way we had hoped.

I'm not sure where you are with your faith. You may not have a relationship with God. You may not believe in the Bible. But if that's true, I'm going to ask you to do me a favor. I'm going to ask you to suspend your judgment. I'm going to ask that you remain open-minded throughout this journey we take together, even though we'll be spending some time in the Bible. You might be surprised where you end up.

On the other hand, you may have grown up in the church. Maybe you've read the Bible all your life, but you've still reached a point where what you thought you knew doesn't seem to be working anymore. You're confused, lost, and possibly annoyed because God hasn't seemed to deliver as so many over the years have promised you he would. I'm praying this journey provides a new perspective on the promises of God. I'm praying you won't jump to the end of some of these stories you've heard a million times but will read with fresh eyes.

You know, I've never heard of anyone's journey of faith that hasn't had a Plan B story—a time in life when a person was going through something completely unexpected. A time when she felt as if God were a long, long, long way away, if he existed at all.

You may be at a critical crossroads in your life where you're trying to find the answer to, "What's next?" or, "Why is this happening?" One thing you probably realize is something has to change. You need some answers. You need to change some patterns. Your hope needs to be renewed.

So who knows? Maybe this journey could be the catalyst for you. The Bible is full of stories about everyday men and women whose plans didn't work out. It's full of people who were trying to figure out what to do with a life that wasn't turning out the way they expected.

People like you.

People who really need hope in the midst of a Plan B.

The Plan B Group Experience

So what do we do with our shattered dreams? What about our unmet expectations? How do we accept our Plan Bs when God doesn't show up the way we thought he would?

While answering these questions together we'll encounter real-life situations and emotions that will challenge us to be real with ourselves, each other, and God. I hope you find the time you spend exploring and sharing your Plan B experiences with your small group to be healing and life changing.

In order to create an environment where each person is free to be authentic and open, it's important to agree on some small group ground rules from the start. Create a "safe zone" for your group. This means that nothing said in the group can be repeated outside the group. Each person's story is his or her own and should only be told by that person. Treating one another with respect and compassion will create a true sense of community that will grow from week to week. In this environment of respect, you should value and protect each other's emotional, spiritual, and physical space; no one should devalue a fellow group member in any way, and no one can be physically touched by another person without permission.

The purpose of your small group is to invite open and honest sharing from your lives, but there are some circumstances that call for limited sharing. Steer clear of sharing anything that will put another person in jeopardy, could lead to legal problems, could reflect poorly on someone else, or you don't have clearance or prior permission to speak about.

Everyone should feel free to share without receiving criticism, advice, or condemnation. You will be on a journey of discovery, telling your own stories and encouraging others to do the same. When someone shares, be sure to thank him for sharing or ask a follow-up question to clarify something he said. Sharing is not an invitation for lecture, correction, or judgment. Make your group an environment of community where each person is encouraged to participate as he or she is able. Avoid letting one person dominate the conversation. Instead, operate according to 1 Corinthians 13:4–7, giving to each other true love, kindness, and patience; bearing, believing, hoping, and enduring all things.

So as we agree to be real with ourselves, each other, and God, let's find out what God has for us. He often does his best work in our most hopeless situations.

HOW TO
USE THIS GUIDE

During your small group time, your group will watch a DVD together that will introduce the main idea and discussion topic for each session. In this guide, you will find that main idea and discussion topic as well as the discussion questions. Your group may not always get through all of the questions in each session. That is just fine. There may be certain questions that hit home with your particular group and will take up the majority of time for that session. The point is not to get through all the questions. Just use these questions as a way to dig deep into each life within your group—your Plan B community. It might help to use your own journal in conjunction with this guide to record any extra notes or thoughts you may have.

This guide includes five days of personal devotions after each session. These devotions are not meant to be homework. They are simply designed to help you continue thinking, meditating, and reflecting throughout the week about what you're experiencing and learning in your small group. Use these devotions to take yourself even further into putting Plan B into action in your own life.

EVERYONE
NEEDS
HEALING

═══ **GROUP DISCUSSION**

GETTING STARTED

Watch DVD session 1.

AFTER THE VIDEO

Shattered dreams. Maybe yours are different from the ones of the lady in our DVD session; her perfectly framed family life didn't turn out the way she expected. But odds are you've experienced at least one shattered dream of your own, if not a number of them. When we think of shattered dreams, we don't have to look far to find examples: failed marriages, desired marriage that never happened, infertility, a disappointing career. Maybe you've been through a traumatic event in your life, or maybe your life just isn't turning out the way you hoped. Some of us have experienced catastrophic events and some of us have not, but regardless, pain, brokenness, and disappointment have affected each of us in some way. Whatever your shattered dream is, the pain of it probably stings a little more each time you see others living your dream. They may seem to have the perfect marriage, perfect kids, or perfect job. But, in reality, each one of those people has also suffered shattered dreams. It's not just you. You are not alone. *Everyone needs healing. Everyone.*

When our deepest dreams and desires seem to die, we're tempted to cry out to God in pain; we feel he is distant and uninvolved as we struggle to deal with sorrow, loss, and doubt. We may feel we have no control over what has happened or is happening to us, and it can lead us to wonder if anyone is in control at all. But what we *can* learn, and hopefully *will* learn, throughout our time together, is broken dreams can be a source of healing and a pathway to eventual growth. In the midst of our Plan B community, we can see God at work in our individual lives and experience God's help when we share with those who care. Together we will begin to understand the connection between crisis and transformation.

So what do you do with a shattered dream? What do you do with an unmet expectation? What do you do when your life isn't turning out the way you thought life was going to turn out? What do you do when you have to turn to Plan B? (*Plan B*, p. 5)

QUESTIONS FOR DISCUSSION

After viewing the session 1 video, discuss these questions with your group.

1. Share a favorite childhood/teenage memory. Maybe you had a great vacation, received an award, or had a really special time with friends or loved ones. What made this one of your favorite memories?

2. What dreams or hopes have you carried with you over the years?

   • Meeting your dream spouse?

   • Having the perfect marriage and/or children?

   • Achieving the ideal job or career position?

   • Other treasured dreams and hopes?

3. What dreams have you given up on?

4. Does it ever seem the world is passing you by? Describe the moments when you have felt passed over or lacking. Has your focus been on your own lack or on someone else's possession of your desires?

5. In your most difficult moments, does it seem true that everyone needs healing? Why or why not?

6. Have you ever experienced being angry at God or deeply disappointed by him? It may have been during a time when you were suffering, sick, dealing with the loss of a loved one, or depressed. How did you feel God let you down?

7. Is there someone in your world you associate with real discouragement? Why? Do you recognize any of that person's characteristics in your own life? Why or why not?

8. Until you can clearly name your loss or shattered dream, you cannot expect to find release or healing. We've learned the first step toward healing is to put a name on that experience or feeling. So with your loss or shattered dream in your mind and heart, consider these questions:

• How will you clearly state the loss or shattered dream?

• What were your missed expectations?

• Why do you think this dream shattered or you suffered this loss?

- How much time has passed since you first felt this loss? Does being separated from the pain for longer periods of time help to blunt the feelings and sense of loss?

- Do you feel that God didn't answer your prayers?

- Do you feel that some good has come from your loss? If so, describe the good you have experienced.

9. We jumped right into the deep end with this session, so you have earned a bit of a breather. Take a moment to consider what we have shared with each other tonight, and then share with the group something that has touched you or helped you in a particular way, and why.

10. Share with the group a specific prayer request relating to or triggered by what you've shared and learned together.

PRAYER

Lord, I live in a broken world full of broken people. But I know that in you I will find the whole and complete healing I need. Help me to name my shattered dreams so I can experience the help and healing you have for me. I desperately need your healing in my Plan B moments. And I thank you for the reality that you show up in unexpected ways and provide as I could never have imagined. Please go with me and the rest of my group throughout this week. Help each of us identify the loss and healing we will encounter in ourselves and others each day. Thank you, Jesus. Amen.

═══ DAY BY DAY

In our session 1 discussion, we faced the reality that everyone needs healing. Reading the Psalms is kind of like entering into the hearts and minds of the writers as they share their innermost thoughts and feelings. They cry out to God in joy and praise, but also in confusion and despair. Even David, a man after God's own heart, experienced moments when he felt God was nowhere to be found.

✳ DAY 1

Psalm 22:1–2: My God, my God, why have you aban-doned me? / You seem far from saving me, / far away from my groans. / My God, I call to you during the day, / but you do not answer. / I call at night; / I am not silent.

Psalm 22:24: [God] does not ignore those in trouble. / He doesn't hide from them / but listens when they call out to him.

Psalm 22:30–31: The people in the future will serve him; / they will always be told about the Lord. / They will tell that he does what is right. / People who are not yet born / will hear what God has done.

Even David had moments when he felt God was distant and removed from his pain. And David wasn't the only one who felt this seeming separation from God. The first few lines of this psalm were uttered by Jesus himself during his agoniz-ing moments on the cross. Jesus felt the pain of separation and cried out to the Father asking why he felt so far away. But the psalm doesn't end with Jesus' question. Instead, a little later in the psalm, we find that David was able to encourage his soul as he remembered the truth about God.

Even though David experienced times of doubt, pain, and insecurity in his walk with God, he still found the faith to believe that, regardless of his feelings and fears, God was listening, not hiding. God was present and involved, not distant and detached. David's heartfelt psalm that began with such confusion and pain actually ends with a positive look toward the future.

Many of us can identify with David. We find ourselves in situations that bewilder us, and we feel as if God has abandoned us. But just as we identify with David in his pain and confusion, can we also identify with him in his trust in God despite the circumstances? Can we learn to experience hope for the future in the midst of our present pain? By following the powerful pattern we see in David's psalm, we can begin to see ourselves, God, and our Plan B from a different perspective. Maybe, just maybe, we too can validate the pain of our current situation while still being able to see a positive future.

QUESTIONS FOR REFLECTION

▸ When was the last time you felt your cries to God went unheard and unanswered? Do you feel that way right now?

▸ In what ways can you find encouragement in knowing that Christ can identify with your pain and confusion?

▶ Why is it important to look toward the future as David did in Psalm 22?

▶ What positive element about your future can you identify right now?

✳ DAY **2**

*Psalm **69:1–3***: God, save me, / because the water has risen to my neck. / I'm sinking down into the mud, / and there is nothing to stand on. / I am in deep water, / and the flood covers me. / I am tired from calling for help; / my throat is sore. / My eyes are tired from waiting / for God to help me.

*Psalm **69:13–17***: But I pray to you, LORD, for favor. / God, because of your great love, answer me. / You are truly able to save. / Pull me from the mud, / and do not let me sink. / Save me from those who hate me / and from the *deep water. / Do not let the flood drown me / or the deep water swallow me / or the grave close its mouth over me. / LORD, answer me because your love is so good. / Because of your great kindness, turn to me. / Do not hide from me, your servant. / I am in trouble. Hurry to help me!*

In Psalm 69, we find David in a situation that should sound familiar to many of us. David felt overwhelmed, as though he were drowning. His throat was sore from crying out and his eyes were weary from searching for answers. David was not sugarcoating his circumstances; he was exhausted, confused, and in need of help. He didn't put on a happy face and try to hide it, but he also didn't thrash around in the floodwaters until they consumed him. Instead, he reached out to God in the midst of his overwhelming reality.

David again did his best to believe that God was bigger than his emotions. It was that belief that caused David to cry out to God in his vulnerability and beg God to save him—and quickly. We can do that too. We don't have to pretend everything is okay. We can cry out to God in our vulnerability; we can beg him to save us. Even when we don't understand, we can look beyond our circumstances just enough to say, "I am in trouble. Hurry to help me!"

QUESTIONS FOR REFLECTION

▸ Can you relate to David's feeling of drowning in his circumstances? What circumstances have threatened (or are threatening) to drown you?

▸ Are you surprised at David's honesty toward God? Why or why not?

▸ How can having the freedom to call out to God honestly, as David did, change the way you deal with life when your Plan A doesn't work out?

✳ DAY **3**

Psalm 31:9–12*: L*ORD*, have mercy, because I am in misery. / My eyes are weak from so much crying, / and my whole being is tired from grief. / My life is ending in sadness, / and my years are spent in crying. / My troubles are using up my strength, / and my bones are getting weaker. / Because of all my troubles, my enemies hate me, / and even my neighbors look down on me. / When my friends see me, / they are afraid and run. / I am like a piece of a broken pot. I am forgotten as if I were dead.*

Psalm 31:21–22*: Praise the L*ORD*. / His love to me was wonderful / when my city was attacked. / In my distress, I said, / "God cannot see me!" / But you heard my prayer / when I cried out to you for help.*

Psalm 31:24*: All you who put your hope in the L*ORD */ be strong and brave.*

This psalm may represent the most tired and truly depressed moment we've experienced with David so far. He had cried so much his eyes ached; his body was filled with grief; he was afraid that not only would he die but he would spend his last moments in tears. He felt weak in every possible way; and on top of all that, he felt that everyone else in the world either hated, looked down on, feared, or had simply forgotten him.

Real pain. Real sadness. Real life. David was filled with more questions than answers. But as we've seen in David's other psalms, this shattered moment was not the end.

Looking back, David remembered God had never failed to come to his aid whenever he cried out, even when it didn't seem probable or even possible. When David recalled God's faithfulness in the past, he experienced renewed hope for the future, even in the face of the most depressing and seemingly hopeless circumstance.

David didn't trust in himself to discover hope for the future. Rather, he turned to what he knew to be true about God. He looked at God's faithfulness and not just his own circumstances. This new perspective gave him the strength he needed, and David encouraged us to do the same.

There is freedom in the realization that we simply can't depend on our own strength. Instead, we can rely on the strength and faithfulness of God. We can recall his steadfast love throughout our lives, focus on his never-changing character, and hold on tightly to the promises that are ours in him, even in the midst of the most challenging situation.

QUESTIONS FOR REFLECTION

▸ Have you ever reached a point of brokenness when you felt out of strength, out of tears, and alone in the world? How did you get there?

▸ How does changing your focus from the reality of your situation to the reality of God's faithfulness help you find strength and hope for the future?

✸ DAY **4**

Psalm 13:1–4: *How long will you forget me, LORD? Forever? / How long will you hide from me? / How long must I worry / and feel sad in my heart all day? / How long will my enemy win over me? / LORD, look at me. / Answer me, my God; / tell me, or I will die. / Otherwise my enemy will say, "I have won!" / Those against me will rejoice that I've been defeated.*

Psalm 13:5–6: *I trust in your love. / My heart is happy because you saved me. / I sing to the LORD / because he has taken care of me.*

Isn't it true that the more we read the Psalms, the clearer it is that Plan B situations are all too common? In this psalm, once again David was worried and sad. His mind was completely preoccupied with all of his troubles. He was dealing with enemies and defeat and just wanted God to look at him. He knew God was his only hope—not only to survive enemy attacks but even just to live his true life. But as always, David was ready to embrace Plan B in the midst of his reality and need for healing.

The idea of singing to God in the midst of our Plan B may not seem very realistic. But when we begin to see the love of God, it is overwhelming and life changing. In the midst of shattered dreams and broken lives, we can still trust in that love. And that trust can be the very thing that will flip our perspective, even to the point of rejoicing. I'm not suggesting that trust is a magical cure that can turn our circumstances into sunshine and roses. But the new light that trust can shed on things can reveal a strength and hope we had forgotten was there.

QUESTIONS FOR REFLECTION

▸ Can you identify with the constant worry and sadness that David expressed in this psalm? In what way?

▸ Do you find it encouraging that one of the most famous people in the Bible had times when he felt he would die if God didn't answer him? If so, in what way? If not, why not?

▶ How do you think David was able to find his trust in God's love? What steps can you take to move toward this kind of trust?

✳ DAY 5

Psalm 142:1–3: I cry out to the Lord; / *I pray to the* Lord *for mercy.* / *I pour out my problems to him;* / *I tell him my troubles.* / *When I am afraid,* / *you,* Lord, *know the way out.*

In session 1, we discussed how we need to name and face our shattered dreams and loss in order to move beyond them. We do that by being honest with God about what we're facing and by sharing it with people who care. David cried out to God and prayed for mercy. But he didn't stop there. He poured out his whole heart to God. He faced and named his loss. He told God his troubles, in spite of his fear. David didn't make light of his situation or pretend that his brokenness didn't hurt. David felt pain, loss, confusion, and despair, just like we do. David faced more than one Plan B in his life. Some of these situations were brought on by his own actions and some by the actions of others. David knew the reality that he needed healing, and he also knew the reality that God is the Healer, even when nothing seems to make sense.

Let's determine to face up to our Plan B situations, to name them, and to realize that our lives are in his hands and we can trust his plan, even when it seems crazy.

Realizing that we're not alone in our need for healing can be such a source of encouragement. Your small group is a community who understands your pain. You can share each other's pain, even when it's hard. God can and will use each of you to strengthen one another.

QUESTIONS FOR REFLECTION

▸ Once you've named your loss, do you find it difficult to ask God for help? Why do you think this is the case?

▸ What is one way you can be honest and pour out your problems to God today?

THE ILLUSION OF **CONTROL**

═══ G R O U P   D I S C U S S I O N

GETTING STARTED

Watch DVD session 2.

AFTER THE VIDEO

Everybody in this group has a different story and has experienced his or her own version of shattered dreams and unmet expectations, but we still have a lot in common. We start life with our own dreams and expectations, and we set out to put our Plan A into motion.

Then, before we know it, life begins attaching strings: marriage, career, children, finances; the list goes on. Our immediate response to those "strings" is often to grab them and try to control the parts of our lives they represent. We try our hardest to control our circumstances and to make our dreams happen according to our Plan A.

But one day, we find ourselves smacked in the face with the unexpected. All those strings we were trying to pull become knotted up and life seems like a big mess. Our Plan A goes spinning out of our control.

This is when we learn that control is just an illusion. Only God can control the circumstances of our lives. What *we can* control is our reaction when our Plan A fails. We may react with anger or fear; we may become bitter with disappointment or try to hide away from life. But that fear, anger, and disappointment will begin to affect every area of our lives: our families, jobs, relationships. We may simply try harder to accomplish our Plan A and in the process turn ourselves inside out and still be no closer to realizing our dreams. In the end, we'll be left with the truth: we are not in control; God is. When our Plan A has come crashing down around us, we must be willing to embrace God's plan.

Your dreams may not be happening, and things may not turn out the way you expected but that doesn't mean your life is spinning out of control. It just means *you're* not in control. (*Plan B*, p. 22)

QUESTIONS FOR DISCUSSION

After viewing the session 2 video, discuss these questions with your group.

1. Share with the group a time when your lack of control resulted in a comedy rather than a tragedy. Maybe you searched for hours for the glasses on top of your head, or maybe you returned to your table at a fancy restaurant with toilet paper stuck to your shoe. How did you respond?

2. In this session we learned the only real control we have is over our reaction to a failed, broken dream. In what ways do you feel your reaction to your failed Plan A has affected other aspects of your life?

3. Has it ever seemed as though your dreams were about to come true, but then you just ended up with dashed hopes? Maybe you lost out on the perfect job. Maybe disaster

ended your dream of the ideal family. Maybe you experienced a broken relationship. Whatever your experience, describe your failed Plan A. What was your reaction?

4. When you think about surrendering to God's plan, what feelings do you experience? Why do you think this is the case?

5. Is there an area of your life right now where you are tempted to control and manipulate something you know you shouldn't?

6. Can you recall a time in your life when God made a dream become a reality in an unexpected way? Describe

the surprising way you saw that dream come true. What truth can you learn from this experience?

7. We learned a bit today about David's struggle with unful-filled dreams. What can you learn from David's experi-ences that may help you accept Plan B in your own life?

| PRAYER

Father, it is so difficult to let go of my own plan for my life and surrender to your Plan B. Please help me learn to stop grasping for control. Help me let go of the anger, pain, disappointment, and fear that have overtaken me and negatively impacted my life. Help me learn to respond to you with a willing heart. I trust you, Lord. Please increase my trust. I ask that you walk closely with me through this week and continue the healing process that will help me to walk freely and joyfully into your Plan B. I ask these things in the name of Jesus. Amen.

══ **D A Y B Y D A Y**

Scripture is filled with examples of people who experienced fear, pain, disappointment, or anger when their dreams seemed impossible; and like us, they reacted in some predictable and some not-so-predictable ways.

When we hear the name Abraham, it's tempting to only think about his successes. He showed some incredible faith in God and became the father of the entire Israelite nation. But Abraham and his family were no strangers to Plan B. They were no strangers to the confusion and frustration and discouragement that come from unfulfilled dreams.

Last week, we took a look at the heart of David and saw his struggle to accept God's plan for his life. This week, let's take a look at Abraham and his family to see what happened when their Plan As fell through, and what we might be able to learn about God and ourselves from their situations.

✴ DAY **1**

Genesis 12:1–2: The Lord *said to Abram, "Leave your country, your relatives, and your father's family, and go to the land I will show you. / I will make you a great nation, / and I will bless you."*

Genesis 12:4: So Abram left Haran as the Lord *had told him, and Lot went with him. At this time Abram was 75 years old.*

Genesis 12:7: *The LORD appeared to Abram and said, "I will give this land to your descendants."*

Genesis 15:2–4: *But Abram said, "Lord GOD, what can you give me? I have no son, so my slave Eliezer from Damascus will get everything I own after I die. . . . Look, you have given me no son, so a slave born in my house will inherit everything I have." Then the LORD spoke his word to Abram: "He will not be the one to inherit what you have. You will have a son of your own who will inherit what you have."*

Genesis 16:1–4, 6: *Sarai, Abram's wife, had no children, but she had a slave girl from Egypt named Hagar. Sarai said to Abram, "Look, the LORD has not allowed me to have children, so have sexual relations with my slave girl. If she has a child, maybe I can have my own family through her." Abram did what Sarai said. It was after he had lived ten years in Canaan that Sarai gave Hagar to her husband Abram. (Hagar was her slave girl from Egypt.) Abram had sexual relations with Hagar, and she became pregnant. When Hagar learned she was pregnant, she began to treat her mistress Sarai badly. . . . Then Sarai was hard on Hagar, and Hagar ran away.*

So what was Abram's Plan A? He had a wife he loved and they wanted to have a family together. He had God's promise that someday he would be the founder of a mighty nation. But after more than a decade, God's promise and the dream of Abram's heart seemed no closer to being fulfilled.

Abram was desperate to live out his Plan A; at his wife's request, he took control and tried to fulfill his own dream. He had a child with his wife's Egyptian slave, Hagar. Sarai, Abram's wife, was jealous of Hagar, and Hagar treated Sarai with contempt. Abram became stuck on the sidelines of an ongoing battle—one that no one could win. The result of Abram's attempt to manipulate life was a wife plagued by anger, fear, and jealousy, and a life filled with strife. His efforts to control his life created a world of problems and solved none.

Most of us have lived some version of this story. Our dreams exist in our hearts and, for a while, we wait patiently for God to bring our dreams to life. Whatever our dreams are, time passes and the dream continues to be just beyond our reach; so we take matters into our own hands and try to control situations, people, or events in order to grasp our dream. We find ourselves living a life that looks nothing like what we've desired. We may find our efforts have pushed our dreams even further out of reach.

It's important for us to remember Abram and Sarai when we are tempted to take control of our lives and try to force our dreams into reality.

QUESTIONS FOR REFLECTION

▶ When can you recall attempting to force your dream into reality?

▶ In what way did the results show you that control is only an illusion?

▶ What lessons have you learned from this experience?

▶ How can you apply these lessons to your efforts to accept God's plan?

✳ DAY 2

*Genesis 17:1, 5–6: When Abram was ninety-nine years old, the L*ORD *appeared to him and said . . . "I am changing your name from Abram to Abraham because I am making you a father of many nations. I will give you many descendants. New nations will be born from you, and kings will come from you.*

Genesis 17:15–18: God said to Abraham, "I will change the name of Sarai, your wife, to Sarah. I will bless her and give her a son, and you will be the father. She will be the mother of many nations. Kings of nations will come from her." Abraham bowed facedown on the ground and laughed. He said to himself, "Can a man have a child when he is a hundred years old? Can Sarah give birth to a child when she is ninety?" Then Abraham said to God, "Please let Ishmael be the son you promised."

Abram and Sarai wanted children desperately. They tried in every way they could to take control of their lives and make it happen. But instead, they only managed to create strife and confusion.

Then God spoke to Abram in his old age, telling him he and Sarai would have a son. God was confirming that he was in control, even in this Plan B moment. And what was Abram's reaction to this wonderful news? Abram laughed and begged

God to please let Ishmael, Hagar's son, be the promised heir. Abram actually tried to convince God to accept and bless his own Plan A.

Abraham's attitude toward the almighty God might seem a bit shocking. But if we're honest, was Abraham's reaction any different than our own when our Plan A is threatened? How often have we pleaded our case to God and tried to convince him that our way is best?

Abraham lived thousands of years ago, but not much has changed when it comes to a failed Plan A. Most of us react a lot like Abraham did—we try with all we have to hang on to our own plans and control our own reality.

QUESTIONS FOR REFLECTION

▸ Has there been a time in your life when you tried to convince God to accept your Plan A? Describe that time.

▸ What emotions did you experience during that time?

▸ How do you now feel when you recall that experience?

▶ What do you believe God might have been saying to you during that time?

✳ DAY 3

*Genesis 18:1–2: Later, the L*ORD *again appeared to Abraham near the great trees of Mamre. Abraham was sitting at the entrance of his tent during the hottest part of the day. He looked up and saw three men standing near him.*

*Genesis 18:9–15: The men asked Abraham, "Where is your wife Sarah?" "There, in the tent," said Abraham. Then the L*ORD *said, "I will certainly return to you about this time a year from now. At that time your wife Sarah will have a son." Sarah was listening at the entrance of the tent which was behind him. Abraham and Sarah were very old. Since Sarah was past the age when women normally have children, she laughed to herself, "My husband and I are too old to have a baby." Then the L*ORD *said to Abraham, "Why did Sarah laugh? Why did she say, 'I am too old to have a baby'? Is anything too hard for the L*ORD*? No! I will return to you at the right time a year from now, and Sarah will have a son." Sarah was afraid, so she lied and said, "I didn't laugh." But the L*ORD *said, "No. You did laugh."*

We've taken a look at Abraham's reaction to God's plan. Now let's focus a bit on Sarah—the ninety-year-old woman who was told she would have a son.

Abraham and Sarah were visited by three heavenly beings, one of whom is referred to as "the LORD." It's a bit difficult to imagine laughing in the face of a promise given by the Lord himself. Yet that is exactly what Sarah did. She not only laughed; she actually made fun of the prophecy. Sarah was so trapped by her own experience and understanding that she could not believe beyond what she could see. For her, any answer outside her own understanding was no answer at all. For her, it seems, "seeing was believing," and what she saw was her own elderly body; all she could focus on were her own unmet expectations and shattered dreams.

Long after Sarah's child-bearing biological clock should have naturally stopped ticking, she still longed to have a child. When her attempt to control her life by encouraging Abraham to have a child through her maid, Hagar, failed to fulfill her desire, the dream of her heart died and all she had left was disappointment and regret. Sarah's pain was so overwhelming she could not even let words of hope from the Lord himself bring relief; she clung to her own failed Plan A even when it meant sorrow and defeat.

It's not hard to imagine Sarah's feelings of hopelessness and resignation. She had done all she could to realize her dream, and her plans had brought only heartache. Now that it seemed to be too late . . . after she had spent a lifetime waiting for her dream to become reality . . . when it was impossible by any earthly means—now she was expected to believe the impossible and accept a totally shocking Plan B.

QUESTIONS FOR REFLECTION

▸ Have you ever had the experience of holding on to your own Plan A long after it had obviously failed? Describe your experience.

▸ What emotions did you have during this time?

▸ In what way can you relate to Sarah's inability to receive words of hope into her sad, discouraged heart?

▶ Were you aware of the presence of a Plan B? What was it? Were you able to accept the relief and hope it offered? Why or why not?

✳ DAY 4

Genesis 21:1–3: The LORD cared for Sarah as he had said and did for her what he had promised. Sarah became pregnant and gave birth to a son for Abraham in his old age. Everything happened at the time God had said it would. Abraham named his son Isaac, the son Sarah gave birth to.

Genesis 21:8–10: Isaac grew, and when he became old enough to eat food, Abraham gave a great feast. But Sarah saw Ishmael making fun of Isaac. (Ishmael was the son of Abraham by Hagar, Sarah's Egyptian slave.) So Sarah said to Abraham, "Throw out this slave woman and her son. Her son should not inherit anything; my son Isaac should receive it all."

Genesis 21:14–15, 16: Early the next morning Abraham took some food and a leather bag full of water. He gave them to Hagar and sent her away. Carrying these things and her son, Hagar went and wandered in the desert of

Beersheba. Later, when all the water was gone from the bag, Hagar put her son under a bush. . . . She sat there and began to cry.

Genesis 21:17–18: *God heard the boy crying, and God's angel called to Hagar from heaven. He said, "What is wrong, Hagar? Don't be afraid! God has heard the boy crying there. Help him up and take him by the hand. I will make his descendants into a great nation."*

The drama that played out in the lives of Abraham and Sarah included Hagar, the Egyptian maid. Her son, Ishmael, was actually Abraham's firstborn son. Hagar had taken advantage of that fact and treated Sarah with contempt; she also allowed her son to treat Sarah and Abraham's son, Isaac, badly. Having been a slave, it was most likely a dream of her heart to be treated with respect and to experience freedom in life. Ishmael was her ticket to her heart's desire; he was her way of accomplishing her Plan A.

And Hagar took full advantage of her position as the mother of Abraham's firstborn son. She had every reason to expect that things would go as planned and her son would be his father's heir. However, God had told Abraham that a nation would be built through Isaac, not Ishmael. So Hagar and Ishmael were forced to leave; it seemed all was lost. Hagar's dream shattered and she sat crying in defeat.

But God had another plan for Hagar and Ishmael. Although Ishmael would not take Isaac's place as Abraham's heir, he would indeed be the father of a great nation, just a different one. God's plan brings blessing, but it just may look different than we expect.

QUESTIONS FOR REFLECTION

▸ In order for Hagar and Ishmael to realize their dream of a home and a people, they had to leave behind their Plan A with no clue what the future held. What emotions do you think they experienced? Have you ever had similar feelings? When?

▸ When have you watched a dream shatter just as it seemed to be coming true?

▸ Have you ever felt that someone else had taken your dream away from you? In what way?

▸ What hope can you take from Hagar's and Ishmael's story?

✳ DAY **5**

Genesis 22:1–2: *After these things God tested Abraham's faith. God said to him, "Abraham!" And he answered, "Here I am." Then God said, "Take your only son, Isaac, the son you love, and go to the land of Moriah. Kill him there and offer him as a whole burnt offering on one of the mountains I will tell you about."*

Genesis 22:8–12: *So Abraham and his son went on together and came to the place God had told him about. Abraham built an altar there. He laid the wood on it and then tied up his son Isaac and laid him on the wood on the altar. Then Abraham took his knife and was about to kill his son. But the angel of the LORD called to him from heaven and said, "Abraham! Abraham!" Abraham answered, "Yes." The angel said, "Don't kill your son or hurt him in any way. Now I can see that you trust God and that you have not kept your son, your only son, from me."*

After years of dreaming and attempting to control his own Plan A and failing, Abraham received his greatest desire—Sarah gave birth to Isaac, their long-awaited, promised son. God's plan had brought his dream to reality. But now, it seemed as if God had yet another plan in mind. He asked Abraham to do the unthinkable—to sacrifice his beloved son. As crazy as it seems to think that God would ask something like this, what seems even crazier is that Abraham actually obeyed him.

But Abraham had seen God work in his life. He had watched over the years as God made the impossible possible and, time and again, brought blessing out of chaos and confusion. So Abraham trusted God.

You see, Abraham had learned that God keeps his promises. God had promised that Abraham would be the father of a great nation and that Isaac would be the heir of all God had given Abraham. So Abraham knew God would bring about a plan that would make that promise a reality. He knew that, if it came down to it, God had the power to raise Isaac from the dead or redeem this difficult situation in some way. Abraham was willing to follow wherever God led, even if following would break his heart. God had taught Abraham that his plans were always the source of blessing. Even when Abraham could not see, he believed. He focused not on his pain but on the goodness of God. And God kept his promise. Isaac lived, and Abraham went on to be the father of a great nation.

QUESTIONS FOR REFLECTION

▸ With which of these people do you most relate: Abraham, Sarah, Hagar, Ishmael, or Isaac? Why?

▸ Has it ever seemed God provided your desires in a way you did not expect, only to have your dream shattered once again? Describe your experience.

▸ In looking back on your life, what instances can you name when God proved to you that he can be trusted?

▸ What promises that God has given you in his Word can you hold to as you learn to accept his plan?

▸ What truth has impacted you the most this week?

WHAT IS **GOD** DOING?

G R O U P   D I S C U S S I O N

GETTING STARTED

Watch DVD session 3.

AFTER THE VIDEO

We've all faced situations when change has disrupted our lives, taking us to unfamiliar places we'd rather not go. Change means facing new circumstances and being forced to live in the unknown. And the unknown can be frightening. But this idea of change is nothing new. As we just learned, God has been using change to shape and bless his people from the beginning of time. Being in line with Noah, David, Daniel, Esther, Joseph, and Paul is not bad company.

Just as it was for those people, the changes in our lives are usually the result of times of crisis. Crisis and shattered dreams disrupt our lives and force us into the unknown.

Maybe your happy marriage is falling apart or the bottom fell out of your once-stable finances. Or maybe sickness has invaded your once-healthy body. Whatever your crisis is, during these times, you may fear God has abandoned you. Fear, in and of itself, is really not a problem. But fear without faith is a big problem. Fear without faith will eat you alive. If you trust only in God's activity, then crisis can lead you to question God's presence or character. But if you trust in God's identity, crisis can lead you to realize that God is most powerfully present even when he seems most apparently absent.

The issue isn't how you feel in the face of the unknown, but, do you trust that God is with you in the middle of the crisis? When faced with crisis, the ultimate question is this: what would you do if you were absolutely confident that God was with you?

> Fear, in and of itself, is really not a problem . . .
> But fear without faith is a big problem. Fear
> without faith will eat you alive. (*Plan B*, p. 61)

QUESTIONS FOR DISCUSSION

After viewing the session 3 video, discuss these questions with your group.

1. Share a childhood experience in which you had to face the unknown—maybe the electricity went out and you

were left in the dark; maybe you moved to a new town or went to a new school.

2. In more recent times, what crisis have you faced that made you question God's presence or purpose in your life? Why do you believe this crisis caused you to question God's faithfulness? What happened to your faith during this time?

3. If you had been completely confident God was with you, what difference might that trust have made in your response to the crisis?

4. How might having complete confidence that God is with you affect your life today? How can this confidence affect the way you face the unknown in the future?

5. Why do you believe it seems easier to trust in God's activity rather than his identity?

6. What difference would it make to respond to crisis based on who he is instead of what he's done?

PRAYER

Father, thank you for loving us and using the changes of Plan B in our lives. But sometimes change is downright scary and it is so difficult to trust you. We want to see you more clearly. We want to understand who you are even when we can't see what you're doing. Help us to see and truly believe you are with us through all the crises, changes, and unknowns of our lives. Thank you for the chance to experience your presence, even when those times are unexpected or challenging. We praise you because of who you are and we are so grateful that our unknowns are never unknown to you. Amen.

═══ DAY BY DAY

Plan B means change is on its way; and we are not the first to experience the challenges or fears it brings. As we have seen in the last two sessions, many examples of this are found throughout the Bible. We briefly met a few of them in the session 3 video. Now let's take a closer look at some of the crises in their lives, how they responded to the unknown, and how God showed up in their Plan Bs.

✳ DAY 1

Genesis 6:9–14: Noah was a good man, the most innocent man of his time, and he walked with God. He had three sons: Shem, Ham, and Japheth. People on earth did what God said was evil, and violence was everywhere. When God saw that everyone on the earth did only evil, he said to Noah, "Because people have made the earth full of violence, I will destroy all of them from the earth. Build a boat of cypress wood for yourself. Make rooms in it and cover it inside and outside with tar.

Genesis 6:19–22*: "Also, you must bring into the boat two of every living thing, male and female. Keep them alive with you. Two of every kind of bird, animal, and crawling thing will come to you to be kept alive. Also gather some of every kind of food and store it on the boat as food for you and the animals." Noah did everything that God commanded him.*

Genesis 8:18–19; 9:1*: So Noah went out with his sons, his wife, and his sons' wives. Every animal, everything that crawls on the earth, and every bird went out of the boat by families. . . . Then God blessed Noah and his sons and said to them, "Have many children; grow in number and fill the earth."*

If anyone ever faced the unknown, it was Noah. God told him to build a giant boat in the middle of dry land. Building a boat this size was no small task; Noah probably faced a lot of criticism and frustration. Not only did Noah face the daunting task of building this boat, but he also had to deal with the fact that the world as he knew it was about to end. Talk about change and a huge Plan B. Once Noah entered the ark, he lived every day in the unknown as he and his family simply floated in their giant boat, the only people left alive. But the Flood eventually subsided and they were finally able to leave the boat.

It's easy to think that once the Flood was over, Noah's work was done. Crisis faced and crisis passed. But Noah's Plan B was really just getting started. Once they made it off the ark, there was the small matter of repopulating the entire earth. How's that for some more change? "Okay Noah, go ahead and start the entire human race over with just your family." But we're all here today, so it looks like that worked out too.

We've heard the story of Noah's ark so often that we might be tempted to just treat it like a fairy tale or myth. But it's important to remember that Noah was a real person faced with real crises. He wasn't always perfect, but he was real. And we can learn from his Plan B. Sometimes the changes that come with our Plan Bs will bring us challenges that seem overwhelming. We may not believe that there is any way we could possibly face such daunting circumstances. The pressure may actually feel like the weight of the world is resting on our shoulders (which is probably how Noah felt). And even when we get through one change, there may be another one right there waiting for us as we exit the giant boat of the unknown. We can learn from Noah that the unknowns don't last forever. But God's love does and he has a plan. And as we walk step-by-step through every situation, we can grow in the confidence that God is truly with us in the middle of every change and challenge.

QUESTIONS FOR REFLECTION

▶ When was the last time you faced a Plan B that seemed overwhelming? What changes brought on that Plan B?

▶ Were you completely confident that God was with you during those times? Why or why not?

▶ If you had been completely confident that God was with you, how might you have faced that challenge differently?

▶ What steps can you take to face the next seemingly overwhelming challenge with this confidence?

✳ DAY **2**

Exodus 3:6–7: *"I am the God of your ancestors—the God of Abraham, the God of Isaac, and the God of Jacob." Moses covered his face because he was afraid to look at God. The L*ORD *said, "I have seen the troubles my people have suffered in Egypt, and I have heard their cries when the Egyptian slave masters hurt them. I am concerned about their pain."*

Exodus 3:10–12: *"So now I am sending you to the king of Egypt. Go! Bring my people, the Israelites, out of Egypt!" But Moses said to God, "I am not a great man! How can I go to the king and lead the Israelites out of Egypt?" God said, "I will be with you."*

Moses' life was far from dull. He was born a Hebrew at a time in history when the Hebrew people were slaves in Egypt. As a baby, Moses' life was threatened by the Egyptian king who commanded that all Hebrew babies be put to death. So Moses' mother hid him to save his life, and in an ironic twist of events, the king's daughter found Moses, had compassion on this helpless baby, and adopted him as her own. He grew up as a prince in Egypt. But one day, he witnessed an Egyptian beating a Hebrew man. Moses defended the Hebrew man and killed the Egyptian. Then the bottom dropped out of Moses' life. News of his actions spread and Moses had to run. He ended up living in the desert and beginning a whole new, very different life.

However, just as suddenly as Moses' life of Egyptian royalty was uprooted, so was his quiet, desert life. God appeared to him and told him to go back to Egypt and tell the king to let God's people—the Hebrews—go. In other words, Moses was to demand that the king allow his entire workforce to walk away. By this time, Moses had settled into his new life rather well. He had a wife and a son and a pretty nice routine of taking care of his father-in-law's sheep. But life changed and brought with it some intimidating unknowns. Moses wasn't sure he could handle this unexpected Plan B. But God told him repeatedly, "I will be with you."

Those words enabled Moses to face the task God had given him. That same promise is for us: God will always be with us. When it seems our lives have fallen to pieces around us and we don't know what to do, we can have confidence that we don't face the crisis alone.

QUESTIONS FOR REFLECTION

▸ Can you relate to Moses' doubt? In what circumstances have you thought, *I'm not such a great person; how can I possibly do this?*

▶ Were you able to identify God's presence in this situation? What was the outcome?

▶ What can you learn from that situation to help you remember that God is always with you?

✸ DAY 3

Daniel 6:1–3: Darius thought it would be a good idea to choose one hundred twenty governors who would rule his kingdom. He chose three men as supervisors over those governors, and Daniel was one of the supervisors. The supervisors were to ensure that the governors did not try to cheat the king. Daniel showed that he could do the work better than the other supervisors and governors, so the king planned to put Daniel in charge of the whole kingdom.

Daniel 6:16–17: So King Darius gave the order, and Daniel was brought in and thrown into the lions' den. The king said to Daniel, "May the God you serve all the time save you!" A big stone was brought and placed over the opening of the lions' den. Then the king used his signet ring and the rings of his royal officers to put special seals on the rock. This ensured that no one would move the rock and bring Daniel out.

When we read these two passages, it's obvious that we're missing part of the story. In the first passage, we are introduced to Daniel, who holds a high position in the government. In the next, the king has turned on Daniel and thrown him into a den with a hungry lion. So what happened? Daniel was a Hebrew who was taken into captivity when he was a young man. He watched his own country be destroyed and then was forced to live in a foreign land. But Daniel remained faithful to God, and became respected by those in power. This respect came with a price: the jealousy of others in the government. Because of their jealousy and deceit, things were about to go really wrong, really fast for Daniel.

Daniel's enemies managed to have a law passed forbidding prayers to anyone but the king. This put Daniel in a tough situation. He could pray to God only in secret and save his career and standing, or he could pray to God openly and faithfully, risking prosecution. This is not a situation Daniel deserved or chose, and he had no power to change it. In a moment of time, he went from being head big-shot to chief lion-food, but he knew God was with him. So, totally aware of the consequences, Daniel prayed to God openly. And God was with him.

When we consider Daniel's story, we might be tempted to skip over his crisis and rush forward to his rescue. But let's take a moment to consider the fact that life often brings circumstances we did not cause or choose, but we still have to face them. Daniel's decision may seem easy as we're looking back on it; of course God was with him and of course the lions wouldn't eat him. But Daniel hadn't read his story—he was living it. Daniel actually had to trust God in the face of hungry lions. How many of us can say that? But the truth is, we serve the same God who was worthy of Daniel's trust. We live in a reality that is not always predictable or pretty. But God is always with us in every moment. We can be like Daniel and trust God, knowing nothing takes him by surprise and he is always bigger than our circumstance.

QUESTIONS FOR REFLECTION

▸ Have you ever faced a dangerous or frustrating situation that you didn't ask for? How did it happen?

▶ How difficult was it to focus on being faithful within the situation rather than to focus on how unfair the situation was?

▶ How does knowing that God is with you help you face circumstances that are undeserved, yet very real?

✳ DAY 4

Esther 4:13–16: Then Mordecai sent back word to Esther: "Just because you live in the king's palace, don't think that out of all the Jewish people you alone will escape. If you keep quiet at this time, someone else will help and save the Jewish people, but you and your father's family will all die. And who knows, you may have been chosen queen for just such a time as this." Then Esther sent this answer to Mordecai: "Go and get all the Jewish people in Susa together. For my sake, fast; do not eat or drink for three days, night and day. I and my servant girls will also fast. Then

*I will go to the king, even though it is against the law, and
if I die, I die."*

Esther was a Jewish girl who was raised by a cousin after
her parents died. Like Daniel, Esther was living in exile in a
country that was not her home. The king of this country
was on the hunt for a new queen, and all the beautiful young
women in the land were brought together to compete for the
job. Esther won. She became the new queen, but she had a
secret: no one knew she was Jewish. This was certainly a situation she never planned, and it was about to get even more
bizarre.

There was a high-ranking man in the government who
had a particular hatred for the Jewish people. He had set a plan
in motion to destroy all the Jews in the land. Esther's cousin
discovered the plan and told Esther. She had a choice to make.
She could go to the king without an invitation (which could
mean her death), confess that she was a Jew, and beg him to
save her people. Or she could hide from the situation, in the
seeming lack of God's presence. Interestingly, God's name
is never mentioned in the entire book of Esther. But you see
God's presence everywhere.

Esther's cousin reminded her that help would come from
somewhere and maybe, just maybe, she was in that place,
at that time, for a reason. It took a fearless faith that should
have been beyond her years, but Esther stepped up. She met
with the king and eventually told him everything. He listened

to her. The Jewish people were alerted and allowed to defend themselves. Those who plotted against them met the violent ends they had planned for Esther's people. Because Esther faced and walked through her Plan B moment, her people were saved and we have an example to encourage us to this day.

You may find yourself in more than one circumstance where it feels as though God is nowhere to be found. You may be facing something so unbelievable and surprising that you're not even sure how to react. But just as God's presence was all over the circumstances of Esther, even though his name wasn't mentioned in the book, God's presence is all over your Plan B experiences, even when you can't see it on the surface. The fact that you are where you are for "such a time as this" can remind you that God is with you, and that is exactly why you can take one more step, talk to one more person, cry one more tear, or take one more risk. He is with you, for such a time as this.

QUESTIONS FOR REFLECTION

▸ Can you identify with Esther or her situation? In what way?

▸ What part do you believe the fasting and praying played in Esther's ultimate actions?

▸ What might have been God's purpose for you in such a time as your last Plan B? How about in what you're facing now?

✳ DAY **5**

2 Corinthians 11:23–27: *I have been near death many times. Five times the Jews have given me their punishment of thirty-nine lashes with a whip. Three different times I was beaten with rods. One time I was almost stoned to death. Three times I was in ships that wrecked, and one of those times I spent a night and a day in the sea. I have gone on many travels and have been in danger from rivers, thieves, my own people, the Jews, and those who are not Jews. I have been in danger in cities, in places where no one lives, and on the sea. And I have been in danger with false Christians. I have done hard and tiring work, and many times I did not sleep. I have been hungry and thirsty, and many times I have been without food. I have been cold and without clothes.*

Philippians 4:11–13: *I have learned to be satisfied with the things I have and with everything that happens. I know how to live when I am poor, and I know how to live when I have plenty. I have learned the secret of being happy at any time in everything that happens, when I have enough to eat and when I go hungry, when I have more than I need and when I do not have enough. I can do all things through Christ, because he gives me strength.*

When we think of the apostle Paul, it's not unlikely that we may think mainly of a man used by God to write most of the New Testament. But we may not think of the very real, very difficult life he led. Paul faced danger and death many times; he suffered physical, mental, and spiritual challenges. But Paul also lived in the confidence of God's presence. There were obviously many times when it couldn't have been easy for Paul to believe that God was with him through it all. But something allowed Paul to face each and every situation, no matter how difficult.

This something was the knowledge that God was with him. In Philippians, Paul explained it straight-out. Paul had learned to be satisfied in every situation. Now, if you're like me, this may sound impossible—to be satisfied and happy in every situation. But Paul explained that he did not achieve this contentment through his own determination or strength. It was Christ who gave him this contentment. It was Christ's strength that made it possible for Paul to deal with difficulties and still persevere—even in the midst of hunger, poverty, and pain. Paul wrote that he had learned the secret, and he passed that secret along to us that we might know the same satisfaction he did: "[We] can do all things through Christ, because he gives [us] strength" (Philippians 4:13).

Amazing and unexpected things can happen when we learn to trust this completely.

QUESTIONS FOR REFLECTION

▸ Have you ever felt like Paul, as if your life was just one struggle after another? How so?

▸ Where do you think Paul found the faith and courage to believe God was with him through all those experiences?

▸ Reflect once more on this question: What would you do if you were absolutely confident that God was with you? Is your answer any different today than it was during the small group time introducing session 3? Why or why not?

ME **TOO**

GROUP DISCUSSION

GETTING STARTED

Watch DVD session 4.

AFTER THE VIDEO

In our own ways, we've all felt the pain and confusion Plan B can bring. But often, these experiences also bring a feeling of isolation. Not only do we feel distant from God, but it may seem we're facing our pain alone, cut off from the people in our lives.

Writer Anne Lamott has said that the most powerful sermon in the world consists of two words: *me too.** Knowing that someone else has been where you are and understands your pain can bring encouragement and hope and healing. The connections "Me too" creates between people are deep and strong. They may seem like simple words, but they are

---

* Anne Lamott, quoted in Rob Bell, *Jesus Wants to Save Christians: A Manifesto for the Church in Exile* (Grand Rapids, MI: Zondervan, 2008), 151.

really a description of one of God's greatest gifts—community. However, this gift comes with a big risk: being vulnerable and authentic.

Today's culture (sometimes even the church) is filled with unrealistic expectations, clichéd answers, and judgmental attitudes. So rather than risk vulnerability, we often choose to hide or pretend. We act as if we have it all together when, in truth, our lives are starting to crumble around us. This is when we need the strength of community the most. But if we refuse to be honest and let others see our pain, emptiness, fear, or sin, we can never experience the hope and power of community.

It's not easy to risk sharing your real self, to be honest and real with God and others. But without them you will find yourself focusing on the pain and confusion you're feeling rather than experiencing the comfort and strength God provides through a community that radiates love, acceptance, and hope.

When you're in a Plan B, you need community more than ever. And yet, because of the pain that comes along with a Plan B, it's easy to miss the God-given gift of community. (*Plan B*, p. 122)

QUESTIONS FOR DISCUSSION

After viewing the session 4 video, discuss these questions with your group.

1. What is the most fun group, club, or team you've belonged to? Why?

2. Do you feel you are or have been part of a community? How would you define that community, and what effect did it have in your life? Why or why not?

3. What difference would being in community make in each of the following situations?

   • When it seems everything in your life is falling apart

   • When someone has betrayed or hurt you

- When you are confused by Plan B

- When you are making wrong choices or unwise decisions

- When you are hiding or pretending

4. Are you ready/willing to make the commitment to community? What steps can you take to make this a reality in your life if you haven't already?

PRAYER

Lord, thank you for the gift of community and the hope it provides in the face of pain and confusion. Please give us the ability to be honest and real with the community you've given us. Most of all,

Lord, help us be real in our relationship with you. We need courage to face and admit our limitations and fears. We need your touch, your healing, and your love. Thank you for surrounding us with a community who can be your hands, your voice, and your comfort. Amen.

DAY BY DAY

The New Testament is the story of the church, God's people—his always-growing community. No one had a greater impact on the spread of Christian community than Paul. His life and teachings point toward a life of authenticity, especially within community. Over the next week, we will take a look at some of Paul's teachings and life experiences to see how he risked being real and vulnerable and learned to live a hopeful, healed, and honest life.

☀ DAY 1

2 Corinthians 12:7–10: So that I would not become too proud of the wonderful things that were shown to me, a painful physical problem was given to me. This problem was a messenger from Satan, sent to beat me and keep me from being too proud. I begged the Lord three times to take this problem away from me. But he said to me, "My grace is enough for you. When you are weak, my power is made perfect in you." So I am very happy to brag about my weaknesses. Then Christ's power can live in me. For this reason I am happy when I have weaknesses, insults, hard times, sufferings, and all kinds of troubles for Christ. Because when I am weak, then I am truly strong.

Paul, through numerous missionary trips, helped to establish many churches, like the one at Corinth. Paul could not be physically present with every community, but he always wanted to stay connected with them, helping them to grow and mature. So as the person who introduced these people to Christ and who was seen as a leader, it would have been tempting for Paul to try to hide any weakness.

That's a very human reaction. When others look up to us, it seems logical to try to live up to their opinion of us. We feel pressure to appear as if we have it all figured out and that we're worth their admiration. But Paul does not fall into this temptation. Rather, he decides to be completely vulnerable with this church by sharing with them a very personal, very challenging issue. As a leader, Paul came right out and said, "I am weak." He reminded them that not only was he the man who helped start their community, but he was a member of it. The very message Paul was giving to them—a message of God's mercy and redemption—he needed just as badly. He was not above weakness; he was as in need of God's grace as they were. As a matter of fact, he admitted he found the greatest strength by depending on God when he was at his weakest.

It's difficult to reveal your whole self to your community. You never know what others will think. You may face judgment or ridicule, but you may also discover love and encouragement. There is a risk. But the risk is worth it. God can use the simple words "me too" within your community to bring great healing and support. But no one can say those words to you if you haven't shared what you're going through. Throughout this week, try to learn from Paul and risk being authentic. You may be surprised at the relief and healing that could follow. It's worth the risk.

QUESTIONS FOR REFLECTION

▶ Were you surprised to hear Paul share such a personal struggle as openly as he did? Why or why not?

▶ Why do you think it was important for that community to know Paul faced struggles just like anyone else?

▶ When have you found yourself at your weakest point? How were you able to embrace the strength that God provides in those moments?

▸ What steps can you take to share your true self within this Plan B community?

✳ DAY **2**

Philippians 3:5–7, 9: *I am from the people of Israel and the tribe of Benjamin. I am a Hebrew, and my parents were Hebrews. I had a strict view of the law, which is why I became a Pharisee. I was so enthusiastic I tried to hurt the church. No one could find fault with the way I obeyed the law of Moses. Those things were important to me, but now I think they are worth nothing because of Christ. . . . Now I am right with God, not because I followed the law, but because I believed in Christ.*

Philippians 3:12–15: *I do not mean that I am already as God wants me to be. I have not yet reached that goal, but I continue trying to reach it and to make it mine. Christ wants me to do that, which is the reason he made me his. Brothers and sisters, I know that I have not yet reached that goal, but there is one thing I always do. Forgetting the past and straining toward what is ahead, I keep trying to reach the goal and get the prize for which God called me through Christ to the life above. All of us who are spiritually mature should think this way, too.*

Just as we saw Paul be vulnerable with the Corinthian community about his weaknesses and struggles, we see him here being vulnerable with the church community in Philippi. He reminded them that whatever he accomplished was not about him; it was all about Christ. Paul was not ashamed of the life he lived before Christ. Instead he confessed all and hid nothing. He was open and honest about his past and did not hesitate to admit he had far to go before he could be the person God wanted him to be. He let his community know he could relate to them and knew the struggles they faced—he communicated a very clear, "Me too."

Christ became the focus of Paul's life. As a result, he could dare to be vulnerable with others. The story was no longer about him; it was about Jesus. Paul made the choice to enter into community through openness and honesty, and he calls us to make the same choice. He challenges us to realize connecting with others will bring us the support and encouragement we need to put the past behind, focus on Christ, and look ahead toward all God calls us to be. Strength to continue the journey can be found in saying and hearing, "Me too."

QUESTIONS FOR REFLECTION

▸ Which parts of Paul's story surprised you? Why?

▶ What types of judgmental attitudes do you think Paul might have faced? How do you think he found the courage to keep being authentic with his community?

▶ Was there a time when you realized that what you were living your life for wasn't all it was cracked up to be? Were you able to refocus on what was truly important? If so, how? If not, why not?

▶ How could your Plan B community help you on your journey of wholeheartedly pursuing Christ?

✴ DAY 3

1 Corinthians 12:12–15: *A person's body is only one thing, but it has many parts. Though there are many parts to a body, all those parts make only one body. Christ is like that also. Some of us are Jews, and some are Greeks. Some of us are slaves, and some are free. But we were all baptized into one body through one Spirit. And we were all made to share in the one Spirit. The human body has many parts. The foot might say, "Because I am not a hand, I am not part of the body." But saying this would not stop the foot from being a part of the body.*

1 Corinthians 12:21–27: *The eye cannot say to the hand, "I don't need you!" And the head cannot say to the foot, "I don't need you!" No! Those parts of the body that seem to be the weaker are really necessary. And the parts of the body we think are less deserving are the parts to which we give the most honor. We give special respect to the parts we want to hide. The more respectable parts of our body need no special care. But God put the body together and gave more honor to the parts that need it so our body would not be divided. God wanted the different parts to care the same for each other. If one part of the body suffers, all the other parts suffer with it. Or if one part of our body is honored, all the other parts share its honor. Together you are the body of Christ, and each one of you is a part of that body.*

In this passage, Paul describes a beautiful picture of community. He explains why we can have the confidence and courage to be vulnerable within a true community. You see, we are not just a collection of people with struggles in common. Rather, we are one complete body connected through and by Christ; each person has a unique and important place within that body.

The fear of being open and authentic is much less when we realize we are all different parts of one body. When we understand that we each were created for our own special purpose within the body, it frees us from unrealistic expectations and judgmental attitudes toward others. We were created to be different; not everyone is supposed to be an "eye," and we can't all be an "ear." We don't need to change each other, but we do need to know when any part of our "body" is suffering, not for the purpose of judging or condemning, but for the purpose of caring and healing.

If we're functioning as such a body, then being vulnerable is not only worth the risk, but it's necessary for the body to prosper. Christ formed us as his body for a reason and when we all agree to play our parts and treat others with respect and love, then our community prospers; even when we're facing crazy circumstances, our community prospers. This is why Paul risked being authentic about his weaknesses and struggles. He knew we all have a part to play, and he was willing to play his. Are you?

QUESTIONS FOR REFLECTION

▸ Does thinking about your Plan B community as different parts of a whole body make sense to you? What roles have you seen different people fulfilling?

▸ What part of the body do you feel you are in your Plan B community? Why?

▸ Why do you think we can sometimes focus on the shortcomings of others, even when we're one body?

▸ What steps can you take to focus on being authentic with sharing yourself in your community? How about in your response when others risk being vulnerable with you?

✳ DAY **4**

2 Corinthians 1:3–7: *Praise be to the God and Father of our Lord Jesus Christ. God is the Father who is full of mercy and all comfort. He comforts us every time we have trouble, so when others have trouble, we can comfort them with the same comfort God gives us. We share in the many sufferings of Christ. In the same way, much comfort comes to us through Christ. If we have troubles, it is for your comfort and salvation, and if we have comfort, you also have comfort. This helps you to accept patiently the same sufferings we have. Our hope for you is strong, knowing that you share in our sufferings and also in the comfort we receive.*

This scripture plays out the way the words "me too" can help us in the difficult times. We will all suffer at some point. But God is the God of mercy and comfort; he will always supply when we need it the most. But it doesn't end there. We can take the comfort we receive and pass it along to others when we see them going through similar struggles. We can say, "Me too! I went through what you're experiencing and I know how it feels. Here's what I've learned. This is what helped me—let me share it with you."

It may be that you are in the middle of a Plan B crisis and are desperately trying to keep your head above water, and God brings someone from your community to share the comfort they received when they were in a similar predicament. Next time, you may be the one from your community who reaches out to share the comfort you've received and the lessons you've learned.

In either situation, it is such a gift to simply know you are not alone. You. Are. Not. Alone. Sometimes you are the comforted and sometimes you are the comforter. Thank God that his mercy is big enough and strong enough to sustain us all as we share and grow together—one Plan B at a time.

QUESTIONS FOR REFLECTION

▸ What feelings do the words "me too" inspire in you?

▸ Have you more often found yourself saying those words or hearing those words? Why do you think that's so?

▸ When have you experienced a time when someone was able to reach out to you with comfort or wisdom they had received in a previous similar situation? When have you been able to help someone else with what you learned from a similar situation?

▸ What is one way you can say, "Me too" to someone in your Plan B community this week?

✴ DAY 5

Galatians 4:12–16: Brothers and sisters, I became like you, so I beg you to become like me. You were very good to me before. You remember that it was because of an illness that I came to you the first time, preaching the Good News. Though my sickness was a trouble for you, you did not hate me or make me leave. But you welcomed me as an angel from God, as if I were Jesus Christ himself! You were very happy then, but where is that joy now? I am ready to testify that you would have taken out your eyes and given them to me if that were possible. Now am I your enemy because I tell you the truth?

Galatians 4:19–20: My little children, again I feel the pain of childbirth for you until you truly become like Christ. I wish I could be with you now and could change the way I am talking to you, because I do not know what to think about you.

Here, we find Paul in an unusual circumstance. He praised this community in Galatia for how they previously loved and accepted him. He had been very sick, and they took care of him and treated him well. They didn't make him feel as if he were a burden or as if he needed to put on a show of false strength to impress them. His sickness wasn't easy, but they were there to support him as a true community does.

But then Paul found himself facing a situation where their support seemed to have ended. They had nearly begun treating Paul like an enemy. He had to decide how to participate in this community in difficult circumstances. Paul could have taken a hard line and told them that he was right and they were wrong and ended the relationship. He could have simply told them whatever they wanted to hear, even if it wasn't true, for the sake of peace. But Paul did neither. Paul simply responded in vulnerability and authenticity, telling them he didn't really know what to think. He didn't have the answer. But what he did know is that he loved them, and he wanted them to truly grow in their faith and become more like Christ. He didn't like having these difficult conversations with them, and wished that he didn't have to. But true community requires honesty, and that's what they got from Paul. Even when it was uncomfortable, Paul confessed the truth in love to his community.

There may be times when you find yourself in the middle of an awkward moment in community. There may be a difficult conversation that needs to be had or a time when you simply have to admit you just don't understand what's going on. A strong community can handle the tough conversations. As a matter of fact, just like the other struggles and Plan Bs we've been talking about, these tough times can actually teach the community and help it come out of the situation stronger than anyone thought it could be.

QUESTIONS FOR REFLECTION

▶ Can you identify with Paul's situation? Have you ever experienced a confusing turn in a community? If so, how did you deal with that event?

▶ Why do you think authentic communities have to face some awkward moments?

▶ What have you learned about community that has surprised you the most?

▶ How can you help make your Plan B community one that is not afraid of the tough situations?

UNANSWERED
QUESTIONS

═══ GROUP DISCUSSION

GETTING STARTED

Watch DVD session 5.

AFTER THE VIDEO

I want a chocolate bar. I can already see the bright shining wrapper; I can hear the crinkle of the paper as I tear into it; I can already taste the creamy, rich goodness. I want a chocolate bar! So I take my crisp, green dollar, put it in the brightly lit machine, check for the right button, and hit it with excited anticipation. I wait expectantly for my chocolate bar to drop. But instead, I am rewarded with an artificially flavored rice cake! I did everything right: right amount of money, right machine, right button; wrong reward! What happened?

How often in our lives do we find ourselves in the same position? We do all the right things, make all the right moves, but the reward we expect never appears. We're left holding what we think is a poor substitute and asking God, "What happened?" We've come to God with the attitude that what he can give us is what's most important. We're way more concerned with what he can give us than with who he is. But worshipping him for who he is, and not just what he does, will be what enables us to handle our Plan B situations.

When our Plan A fails and Plan B overtakes us, we must be willing to let go of our dreams and take hold of God's plan for our lives—whether we understand or not. Reality is not as simple as we try to make it. We don't always have the answers, but God is still God. We are called to be faithful and worship him for who he is, even when it seems he is not coming through the way we hoped. Knowing him for who he is will always be more valuable than any dream we could ask him to fulfill.

You may have more questions than answers, but will you still trust God enough to seek him in the middle of your Plan B? Are you willing to abandon your dreams in order to receive the life he has dreamed for you? Can you praise him for your Plan B?

> We're looking for a quick spiritual transaction that doesn't necessarily lead to a deeper level of intimacy but gives us what we want. (*Plan B*, p. 84)

QUESTIONS FOR DISCUSSION

After viewing the session 5 video, discuss these questions with your group.

1. Describe a time in your life when you didn't get what you expected: maybe the vending machine became your enemy, or the jeans you ordered arrived on time but were three sizes too big.

2. In what way have these types of situations affected how you view God? How do you now see him? What are his characteristics, and how have you experienced these in your life?

3. In light of these characteristics of God, why do you think it is often so difficult to trust him in the middle of your Plan B times?

4. Of the words you used above to describe God, how many of them are based on his actions? Why do you think it comes so naturally to describe God in relation to his actions?

5. How would you restate the following thought: *I believe there is a God and it's not me?* How could that impact the way you respond to your Plan Bs?

6. How can you move toward the type of trust in God it takes to seek him with reckless abandon and worship him through your tears?

PRAYER

Dear God, life is difficult. The questions always come and the answers sometimes seem to hide. Please help us understand that nothing hides from you, so we can worship you through all the questions and answers. Please help us to trust you with our lives, even when they seem dark and lonely. Help us to remember who you are so we will have the courage to continually seek you, even when life is overwhelming us. You are not overwhelmed. You are not shaken. You are the source of our lives and the author of our dreams. Help us to dream with you. We praise you for who you are and thank you for what you've done. Amen.

====== DAY BY DAY

Praising God for who he is and not just what he does sometimes means we will have to praise him and serve him, even through our tears. Each week we've seen examples of people through biblical history who have had to deal with Plan B situations. This week, we're going to see examples of people who chose to praise God, even through their tears. Through their stories, we can learn about ourselves and our relationship to the God who loves us through every circumstance.

✳ DAY 1

1 Samuel 1:2, 6, 10–18: Elkanah had two wives named Hannah and Peninnah. . . . Peninnah would tease Hannah and upset her, because the LORD had made her unable to have children. . . . Hannah was so sad that she cried and prayed to the LORD. She made a promise, saying, "LORD All-Powerful, see how sad I am. Remember me and don't forget me. If you will give me a son, I will give him back to you all his life, and no one will ever cut his hair with a razor. While Hannah kept praying, Eli watched her mouth. She was praying in her heart so her lips moved, but her voice was not heard. Eli thought she was drunk and said to her, "Stop getting drunk! Throw away your wine!" Hannah answered, "No, sir, I have not drunk any wine or beer. I am a deeply troubled woman, and I was telling the LORD *about all my problems. Don't think I am an evil woman. I have been praying because I have many troubles and am very sad." Eli answered, "Go! I wish you well. May the God of Israel give you what you asked of him." Hannah said, "May I always please you." When she left and ate something, she was not sad anymore.*

Meet Hannah. Hannah had much to be thankful for in her life, but she also had a heartache: she could not have children. As if the pain of the impossible dream in her heart was not enough, she also had to deal with her husband's other wife, who used Hannah's deepest pain against her. Hannah had a decision to make. She could have chosen to give in to the bitterness of an unfulfilled dream. She could have given up on her dream altogether, as if it never mattered, simply hiding the truth. But Hannah did neither.

Hannah shed honest tears. She chose to cry out her pain to God. She cried and prayed so intensely that Eli, the priest, thought she was drunk. But Hannah was not drunk; she dared to trust God enough to praise him, even when her heart was broken. She was willing to trust him with her life and that of her hoped-for child. Hannah walked away from that moment with a lighter heart. Hannah finally did get the child she prayed for so intensely. But she received comfort even before her prayers for a child were answered.

Maybe you can relate to Hannah exactly. Maybe there is a dream in your heart that you have desperately wanted to come true. Maybe you have had to watch someone else in your life live out the dream you had dreamed for yourself. Maybe you are at the point where you have to decide what to do with your tears. Will you cry them in a steady stream of bitterness? Will you dry them up and hide them behind a wall of fake indifference? Or will you cry them honestly, praising God through them? Will you trust the goodness of God's character even though you don't understand your circumstance? When you can praise God through your tears, you can be comforted by the truth of his character whether you receive your desire or not.

QUESTIONS FOR REFLECTION

▸ How can you relate to Hannah and her situation?

▶ In what ways have you faced situations that left you at the point of painful tears? Were you able to praise God through the tears?

▶ Does it surprise you that Hannah walked away from Eli not feeling sad anymore, even before she became pregnant? Why do you think that horrible sadness left her?

▶ What has discouraged you from crying out to God through the tears of an unrealized dream? How can you find the courage to praise God even through the tears?

✳ DAY 2

> **Lamentations 3:17–26**: *I have no more peace. / I have forgotten what happiness is. / I said, "My strength is gone, / and I have no hope in the LORD." / LORD, remember*

my suffering and my misery, / my sorrow and trouble. / Please remember me / and think about me. / But I have hope / when I think of this: / The Lord's love never ends; / his mercies never stop. / They are new every morning; / Lord, your loyalty is great. / I say to myself, "The Lord is mine, / so I hope in him." / The Lord is good to those who hope in him, / to those who seek him. / It is good to wait quietly / for the Lord to save.

Jeremiah had plenty of reasons for tears. He is actually often referred to as "the crying prophet." He saw the coming destruction of his own country and could not stop it. He had to experience firsthand the utter devastation of his homeland and the suffering and deportation of his people. The demolition of his city, Jerusalem, was so complete there was no food to be found. Jeremiah said that those who were killed in the war were better off than those who were starving to death. Pain, suffering, and need were everywhere he looked.

But he was able to look beyond these circumstances, through his tears, and see the truth about God. The circumstances surrounding him could have been blinding, but even through the immense pain, Jeremiah was able to see God's identity. Through the haze of war and destruction, Jeremiah recalled and trusted in God's character—his love and mercy and goodness. And that gave Jeremiah hope in the midst of tragedy.

There may be a time when you will face destruction in your own life. It may not look like the downfall of Jerusalem, but the foundation of your life might seem in shambles. There may not be any single action you can identify as positive or encouraging. But, like Jeremiah, you can look beyond your circumstances toward the truth of God's character: his love and mercy and goodness. Because of God's proven faithfulness, even when things are in shambles, you can recognize who he is, cry honest tears, and trust him. Jeremiah did eventually receive beautiful promises from God about the restoration of Jerusalem. And you will see restoration in your life as well. When you can trust God through your tears of pain, it makes the tears of restoration that much sweeter.

QUESTIONS FOR REFLECTION

▸ In what ways have you felt that your life was in shambles? What brought this about?

▸ How did you handle that crisis? Were you able to glimpse any future restoration in the destruction?

▶ Why do you think Jeremiah chose to praise God for his character, and not just his actions? Are you able to look past actions that confuse you in order to trust God's identity? How so?

▶ In what ways can you train yourself to look past circumstances into the truth of God's character?

✳ DAY 3

Isaiah 38:1–6*: At that time Hezekiah became very sick; he was almost dead. The prophet Isaiah son of Amoz went to see him and told him, "This is what the L*ORD* says: Make arrangements, because you are not going to live, but die." Hezekiah turned toward the wall and prayed to the L*ORD*, "L*ORD*, please remember that I have always obeyed you. I have given myself completely to you and have done what you said was right." Then Hezekiah cried loudly. Then the L*ORD* spoke his word to Isaiah: "Go to Hezekiah and tell him: 'This is what the L*ORD*, the God of your* *ancestor David, says: I have heard your prayer and seen your tears. So I will add fifteen years to your life. I will save you and this city from the king of Assyria; I will defend this city.'"*

Hezekiah was the king of Judah and it appeared he and his people were about to be overtaken by an enemy nation. As if this weren't challenging enough, a prophet of God told Hezekiah that he would soon die. This was a time of tears for Hezekiah. His nation was going down and he was going down with it. But Hezekiah, like Hannah and Jeremiah, chose to see beyond his tears. Instead of choosing to quit, he trusted that God, in his faithfulness, would hear him when he cried out. So Hezekiah did just that; he cried out to God and God did hear him. Not only did Hezekiah live fifteen more years, but Judah survived the attack.

While you may not be a wartime king, odds are good that you have faced situations that seemed overwhelming. Maybe it was the loss of a job or the betrayal of a friend that made it seem it would be easier to just quit. Maybe you received an answer from God rather quickly, as Hezekiah did. Or maybe you had to wait. Maybe you're still waiting.

We don't always get the immediate answer the way Hezekiah did. But it's important to remember that Hezekiah didn't know the answer would come fast when he cried out to God. He chose to praise God through the tears and to trust in his goodness. And that's what we can learn from Hezekiah:

no matter how intimidating the news we get or the challenge we face and no matter how quick or slow the answer may come, we can choose to trust through the tears.

QUESTIONS FOR REFLECTION

▶ What were Hezekiah's options for response when he got the message from Isaiah? Why do you think Hezekiah chose to cry out to God?

▶ What do you think Hezekiah learned from this experience? How so?

▶ What makes it so difficult to cry out to God through your tears? How can you prepare yourself to respond like Hezekiah the next time you're faced with Plan B?

✳ DAY **4**

***John 11:1–2**: A man named Lazarus was sick. He lived in the town of Bethany, where Mary and her sister Martha lived. . . . Mary's brother was Lazarus, the man who was now sick. So Mary and Martha sent someone to tell Jesus, "Lord, the one you love is sick."*

***John 11:17, 20–27**: When Jesus arrived, he learned that Lazarus had already been dead and in the tomb for four days. . . . When Martha heard that Jesus was coming, she went out to meet him, but Mary stayed home. Martha said to Jesus, "Lord, if you had been here, my brother would not have died. But I know that even now God will give you anything you ask." Jesus said, "Your brother will rise and live again." Martha answered, "I know that he will rise and live again in the resurrection on the last day. Jesus said to her, "I am the resurrection and the life. Those who believe in me will have life even if they die. And everyone who lives and believes in me will never die. Martha, do you believe this?" Martha answered, "Yes, Lord. I believe that you are the Christ, the Son of God, the One coming to the world."*

***John 11:38–41; 43–44**: Again feeling very upset, Jesus came to the tomb. It was a cave with a large stone covering the entrance. Jesus said, "Move the stone away." Martha,* *the sister of the dead man, said, "But, Lord, it has been four days since he died. There will be a bad smell." Then Jesus said to her, "Didn't I tell you that if you believed you would see the glory of God?" So they moved the stone away from the entrance. . . . "Lazarus, come out!" The dead man came out, his hands and feet wrapped with pieces of cloth, and a cloth around his face.*

Lazarus and his two sisters were close friends of Jesus. He loved them. That's why it seemed particularly confusing to Mary and Martha that Jesus didn't arrive to help Lazarus before he died. Jesus didn't show up when or how they expected, but he did show up. Martha could have blamed Jesus for her grief. She could have railed at him in a fit of rage. She could have given herself over to the numbness of grief and shut herself off from Jesus. Instead, when Martha heard Jesus had arrived, she went right out to meet him. She opened her heart to him and cried out her pain and confusion. Even though Jesus had not acted in a way she had hoped or understood, she still confessed that he was her Lord. She still expressed her full belief and trust in him. She was able to look beyond the actions she didn't understand to believe in the character she knew.

In the middle of grief, it can be extremely difficult to see anything beyond your pain. You may see a desolate life with nothing but miles of disappointment and loss stretching out in front of you. But it doesn't have to end there. Martha was able to keep believing in who she knew Jesus to be. And in just a little while, she got her brother back in a way she never expected. I can't tell you that your answer will come that soon or that miraculously. But I can tell you that if you see past your pain to the truth of who Jesus is, and praise him even through your tears, you'll find that he will show up. It may not be when, where, or how you expect it, but he will show up and bring hope and comfort to your broken heart.

QUESTIONS FOR REFLECTION

▸ What thoughts do you think were going through Martha's mind when she was waiting on Jesus to come to them?

▸ Were you surprised at Martha's conversation with Jesus? Why or why not?

▸ How do you think Martha found the faith to believe and confess Jesus' identity even when his actions confused her?

▸ What can you learn from Martha that can help you see beyond your own pain and praise God through your tears?

✳ DAY 5

Luke 22:39–44: Jesus left the city and went to the Mount of Olives, as he often did, and his followers went with him. When he reached the place, he said to them, "Pray for strength against temptation." Then Jesus went about a stone's throw away from them. He kneeled down and prayed, "Father, if you are willing, take away this cup of suffering. But do what you want, not what I want." Then an angel from heaven appeared to him to strengthen him. Being full of pain, Jesus prayed even harder. His sweat was like drops of blood falling to the ground.

Even Jesus Christ himself knows the pain of crying out to God through his tears. Jesus is God; he came to earth as fully God *and* fully human to save us and provide us with his life. But this would involve the most massive physical, emotional, and spiritual pain that can be imagined. As Jesus prayed in the garden just before his death, he was under so much stress that the tears in his eyes weren't enough. It was as if his whole body needed to cry out—"His sweat was like drops of blood." Jesus knew exactly what he was facing, and he even knew why he was facing it. He chose to! Yet he still cried out in the honesty of his heart. He begged the Father for another way, if at all possible. But he knew the Father's heart of love, and he ultimately was willing to face the pain and follow through on his plan to save us.

Our Savior can identify with our pain and our struggles. And now we can live in his grace and mercy. Because Jesus faced down all our sin and death and shame, we can face up to any Plan B. Even when we wish there were some other way, we know that he is Lord of all ways and that we can trust him to act perfectly because we know his perfect love.

QUESTIONS FOR REFLECTION

▸ Why do you think Jesus prayed for another way?

▸ Why do you think Jesus asked his disciples to pray at the same time?

▶ How does it make you feel to know that Jesus himself can identify with you in the middle of your pain?

▶ In what ways can you continue to focus on who God is, even when you're confessing this through your tears?

THE **CROSS**

GROUP DISCUSSION

GETTING STARTED

Watch DVD session 6.

AFTER THE VIDEO

If anything has become clear during our time together, it's that trouble comes to us all. Rich, poor, man, woman, young, old; there's no getting around it. Even Jesus told us straight out, "In this world you will have trouble" (John 16:33). There's no plainer way to say it. I bring this up not to depress you, but to remind you of something more important—trouble is not the end of the story. Though trouble is inevitable, Jesus offers hope with these powerful words: "But be brave! I have defeated the world" (v. 33).

If we lived in television land, all our problems would be wrapped up in thirty minutes with a nice little bow of resolution, and we could go on, thankful for the encouragement in the second half of the verse. But we don't live in that world.

There is not a bow that will tie up all the loose ends of our Plan Bs before our time together ends. So instead of just giving you the second half of that verse and telling you to "buck up," I want to take you to the source of that verse—to the place where the pain of trouble meets up with the victory of over-coming. That place is the cross. In the middle of Plan B, you may feel God doesn't love you or doesn't care. But at the foot of the cross, you clearly see the truth: God does love you and God does care. So much so that he sacrificed himself for you— so you could have eternal life. And not only in the future, but also today, here in this world. He has given you a way to have hope in the middle of difficult times and an anchor to hold you steady when the world around you is rocking uncontrollably.

Sometimes we forget about this great love and this strong anchor. We settle into a mediocre life, distracted by the day-to-day, never becoming the persons God intends for us to be. It's often in these times of busyness and distraction that Plan B will come. We are suddenly rocked out of our settled exis-tence and not sure what to do next. But the cross is still there. It is still the anchor. It is still our hope. Because of the victory of the cross, God can take the pain of our Plan Bs and make something beautiful. While we're lingering in the questions and the waiting, God can speak clearly and honestly straight into our hearts and souls.

We don't have a pretty bow to wrap around this study, but we have something infinitely better. We have the cross. We have the victorious God who can bring beauty from ashes, who can bring meaning from every circumstance and provides us with an anchor in the middle of any storm. So in the midst of our pain, let us recognize and embrace the beauty God is creating in us and let us hold on tight and never lose hope; never lose sight of the cross.

> Do you know what the most frequently stated promise from God in Scripture is? God promises us over and over: "I am with you." (*Plan B*, p. 208)

QUESTIONS FOR DISCUSSION

After viewing the session 6 video, discuss these questions with your group.

1. In what ways have you seen God's love in action during this past week?

2. What has most surprised you about yourself in this study? About God? About others?

3. What Plan B are you now facing? How has this study affected the way you are dealing with your Plan B?

4. What change, meaning, or purpose do you believe God has in mind for your Plan B? How can you work with him in this process of change?

5. How have the stories of others in your Plan B community helped or challenged you?

6. Has the cross of Jesus been an anchor of hope for you in the midst of your Plan B? If so, how?

7. As we reach the end of this study, as we stand at the foot of the cross, what do you hear God speaking to your heart?

PRAYER

My Savior, how do I thank you for the cross? How do I express my gratitude for the love you pour out for me? Help me to trust you when I don't understand, and hold to your hope when my life is shaken. I know trouble will come, but help me hold to your promise and truly believe you have already overcome. Help me to remember that everyone needs healing. I thank you, Lord, for this community and the way you've used us in one another's lives. Help me to remain open to others as this group ends; lead me to others who need your touch in their own Plan B; use me to be a source of your love and healing in the lives of your people. I thank you for your love; without it we could do nothing. Because of your love, we trust you will bring beauty from our Plan Bs. In the name of our Lord, Jesus, I pray. Amen.

═══ DAY BY DAY

Have you ever considered all Jesus did for you when he died on the cross? He paid the penalty for sin, so you would not have to die; but he did so much more.

The foot of the cross is where we find life. The foot of the cross is where we find love. The foot of the cross is where we find the courage to believe and the anchor to hold us firm when the world goes crazy. As we approach the end of this study, let's approach some other people we find at the foot of the cross. Each of these people was faced with a Plan B moment. Let's see how they reacted and what we can learn from their experiences.

✳ DAY 1

> **John 19:25–27**: *Standing near his cross were Jesus' mother, his mother's sister, Mary the wife of Clopas, and Mary Magdalene. When Jesus saw his mother and the follower he loved standing nearby, he said to his mother, "Dear woman, here is your son." Then he said to the follower, "Here is your mother." From this time on, the follower took her to live in his home.*

Mary loved Jesus with the love only a mother could have. From the moment the angel Gabriel told her Jesus would come into her life, her life was never the same. She watched him grow and learn and minister and heal. She saw him laugh and love and pray. And then she stood by, watching her son die. The amazing divine plan that had drawn her in over thirty years before seemed to be ending too soon, and too tragically. Even through his intense suffering, and the burden of carrying all sin, for all time, Jesus took a moment and looked directly at her.

Jesus reached out in love during his most painful moment to speak to his mom one more time. He showed her his love one more time by entrusting her care to a loved and trusted friend. In the most painful moment of her life, Mary got a personal, loving moment with the Savior.

You can find that same love, compassion, and care when you meet Jesus at the cross. In the midst of your despair, he can look at you and show you his mercy. You will have moments when your heart aches and all seems lost, but the cross is the place where you can meet the ultimate love that will be with you through every heartbeat, every tear, and every smile.

QUESTIONS FOR REFLECTION

▶ What thoughts and feelings do you think Mary was dealing with at the cross?

▶ What kind of love does it take to think of someone else's pain when you're in the midst of your own?

▶ Why do you think Jesus chose that moment to speak to his mother's care?

▶ How does it feel to know that Jesus was showing his love for you at that moment as well? How does it feel to know that because Jesus faced and overcame death at that cross, you can now face your Plan B with hope?

✴ DAY 2

John 19:25–27: *Standing near his cross were Jesus' mother, his mother's sister, Mary the wife of Clopas, and Mary Magdalene. When Jesus saw his mother and the follower he loved standing nearby, he said to his mother, "Dear woman, here is your son." Then he said to the follower, "Here is your mother." From this time on, the follower took her to live in his home.*

You may notice that this is the same Scripture passage as yesterday. That's not a mistake. We're going to think about this passage again, but from a slightly different angle. Yesterday, we thought about how Jesus expressed his love to his mother from the cross. But for just a moment, let's think about the man to whom Jesus entrusted his mother's care.

When Jesus was arrested, his followers and friends were scared. They basically abandoned him in fear and confusion. But the disciple Jesus loved didn't stay gone for long. He came back to be there for his best friend, to be with his friend in his final moments. We can't help but wonder if he had guilt lingering in his heart. Did he wish he had been more faithful? Did he wonder if Jesus still loved him or trusted him? Did he feel worthy of love or trust?

We can only guess what he may have been feeling. But we don't have to guess about Jesus. Jesus looked him in the eye and trusted him to care for his very own mother. Jesus showed him love and trust and compassion, even while he was suffering torture and near death. The disciple found incredible, forgiving, accepting, and healing love at the foot of the cross; the same love we can find there for ourselves. Even if we don't feel worthy of it; even if we feel guilty; even if we know there's no way on earth we deserve that kind of love and forgiveness—Jesus proved his love from the cross and offers it to us still. None of us is worthy of it, but that's the message of the cross. He freely died so we could live. The cross is all about Jesus and his love for you! Even when you feel too dirty or too cynical or too guilty for the foot of the cross, remember this disciple. Jesus will pour out his love and forgiveness whenever we come to him.

QUESTIONS FOR REFLECTION

▸ Have you ever felt as though you were too guilty to meet Jesus at the cross? What made you feel that way?

▸ How does it feel to know that Jesus has overcome every obstacle between you and the cross because of what he did on the cross?

▸ When was the last time you truly believed that Jesus loved you? How might your Plan B reactions be different if you completely believed that he loved you, no matter what?

✳ DAY **3**

> **Mark 15:31–32**: *The leading priests and the teachers of the law were also making fun of Jesus. They said to each other, "He saved other people, but he can't save himself. If he is really the Christ, the king of Israel, let him come down now from the cross. When we see this, we will believe in him."*

The leading priests and teachers of the law were generally not friends or fans of Jesus. Jesus' revolutionary teaching of love and salvation threatened their organized religious traditions, so they saw him as an enemy. Their desire to have Jesus taken out of the picture in the most drastic way possible was finally coming true, but they weren't content just to watch. They had to be there and participate. They mocked him and did everything they could to point out how all his claims to be the Messiah must have been false, since he couldn't even save himself from this torture and death.

You may wonder exactly how to relate to people like this. But the truth is, we were all like them at some point. We were all sinners and we all needed to be saved by the love Jesus showed on the cross. Jesus died for all our sins, including theirs. Think about that: while they made fun of him and participated in his humiliation, he was enduring it all so that he could save them, so that they could one day accept his love and salvation. Jesus prayed to the Father to forgive them and was at that moment making that forgiveness possible.

When we read about the priests and teachers mocking Jesus at the cross, we can be reminded again of the strength of his love. His love is strong enough to forgive and save even those who mocked him to his face. His love is strong enough to reach us at our most shameful and messed-up moment. And his love is strong enough to meet us and walk with us through our Plan Bs.

QUESTIONS FOR REFLECTION

▸ What do you think Jesus felt when he endured all the mocking around him?

▸ When have you felt the strength of Jesus' love?

▸ How can the great love Jesus showed at the cross make it the anchor for our lives?

✳ DAY **4**

> *Matthew 27:50–51, 54: But Jesus cried out again in a loud voice and died. Then the curtain in the Temple was torn into two pieces, from the top to the bottom. Also, the earth shook and rocks broke apart. . . . When the army officer and the soldiers guarding Jesus saw this earthquake and everything else that happened, they were very frightened and said, "He really was the Son of God!"*

The army officers and soldiers at the foot of the cross were not as familiar with Jesus as the religious leaders and teachers we met yesterday. To them, Jesus was an outcast Jewish rabbi who had been stirring up trouble among the people. To them, he most likely appeared to be like any other criminal they had executed. But it did not take too long for even these soldiers to realize Jesus was no ordinary man.

The Creator physically entered creation and then was put to death. Creation had to revolt against such a travesty. And it did. The sky responded with darkness and the entire earth shook violently. This was no ordinary earthquake and the timing was no coincidence. Something huge happened at the scene of Jesus' death and the soldiers could not deny it. They knew at that moment that Jesus was who he said he was; he was truly the Son of God.

There will be times, many of them during our Plan Bs, when God shows up so powerfully and so obviously that there is no doubt to anyone watching that something miraculous has happened. When we can continue to walk with God through our Plan B moments, who knows what amazing things other people can see from our situations. Let's pray that it doesn't always take an earthquake to show the power of the cross, but let's show the power of the cross in our lives, even in the simple things, so that others can look at what's going on and say that the only explanation is that Jesus is the Son of God!

QUESTIONS FOR REFLECTION

▸ What do you think the soldiers did after they realized who Jesus really was?

▸ Have you ever experienced any "earthquake" times in your life, when God worked in such a big way that there was no denying him? How did that affect the people in your life?

▸ Have you ever experienced God working in a quieter and subtler way? How did it feel to know God was working, even in a still, calm way?

▸ How can you let your Plan B experiences help others come to know Jesus' love?

✸ DAY 5

Luke 23:32–34: *There were also two criminals led out with Jesus to be put to death. When they came to a place called the Skull, the soldiers crucified Jesus and the criminals—one on his right and the other on his left. Jesus said, "Father, forgive them, because they don't know what they are doing."*

Luke 23:39–43: *One of the criminals on a cross began to shout insults at Jesus: "Aren't you the Christ? Then save yourself and us." But the other criminal stopped him and said, "You should fear God! You are getting the same*

*punishment he is. We are punished justly, getting what
we deserve for what we did. But this man has done nothing wrong." Then he said, "Jesus, remember me when you
come into your kingdom." Jesus said to him, "I tell you the
truth, today you will be with me in paradise."*

Trouble had come to the robbers on the two crosses beside
Jesus. This was trouble they had invited, but it was trouble
nonetheless. One thief chose to lash out at Jesus in the middle of his consequences. Jesus was the one person who could
save him—who was literally dying to save him—and yet he
couldn't see it. He let his bitterness color the last interaction
he had on earth with the One who could have made all the
difference.

But the other robber was a different story. He faced up to
his situation—what he had done and the consequences he
was enduring. He didn't let bitterness overtake his attitude.
Instead, he focused on who Jesus was and his relationship to
him. He dared to ask Jesus to remember him when he came
into his kingdom; and Jesus was, at that very moment, making
his request possible. Jesus' love was already saving him; it was
already reaching down and out from the cross and embrac-
ing his mother, his disciple, and this robber. And Jesus' love is
still reaching out today. It is anchored in the heart of God and
shown to us through the cross, our anchor in a topsy-turvy
world.

No matter what your Plan B situation is, you can overcome the bitterness and the pain and the cynicism you might be tempted to feel. You can look to Jesus and confess who he is and thank him for including you in his kingdom. You can thank him for overcoming this world so that you can face every situation with a faith and a hope that is real and solid. There will be trouble, but he has overcome. Praise him!

QUESTIONS FOR REFLECTION

▸ In what ways has Jesus helped you overcome your Plan B issues?

▸ How does it feel to know that Jesus' love was reaching out to you from the cross, ready to save you because of his sacrifice?

▸ When the trouble you face begins to overwhelm you, how can the cross be your anchor?

▸ What is the most surprising thing you learned about yourself in this study of Plan B? What is the most surprising thing you have learned about God?